1. 99

Small engines can use tracks that weave between the flowerbeds in a garden. This view shows a train on the 7¹/₄″ gauge Woodbine Cottage Garden Railway (P).

Miniature Railways
Michael Crofts

A Shire book

Published in 2002 by Shire Publications Ltd,
Cromwell House, Church Street, Princes Risborough,
Buckinghamshire HP27 9AA, UK.
(Website: www.shirebooks.co.uk)

British Library Cataloguing in Publication Data:
Crofts, Michael
Miniature railways. – (A Shire album; 405)
1. Railroads, Miniature – Great Britain
I. Title
625.1'9'0941
ISBN 0 7478 0529 6

Cover: *A train on the 10¼" gauge railway at Audley End in Essex, driven by the railway's owner, Lord Braybrooke.*

ACKNOWLEDGEMENTS
I acknowledge with gratitude all those who have filled gaps in my knowledge or provided other assistance, including George Barlow, Robin Butterell, Paul Conibeare, Mary Culver, David Curwen, John Dutton, Don Fifer, Lieutenant Commander Roy Francis, Colin Healey, Dave Holroyde, Marc Humphreys, Alex Hurd, Peter Johnson, Neville Knight, Roderick McCrea, Andrew Neale, Chris Rennie, Brian Rogers, Owen Ryder, Adrian Sant, Peter Scott, Neil Simkins, the Stirland family, Ian Thomas, Simon Townsend, Peter van Zeller, James Waterfield, Rodney Weaver, John Williams, and the members of the discussion egroup called *UKminiaturerailways*. I apologise if I have left anyone out. Any errors are mine alone. I am also grateful to the owners of private miniature railways who have allowed me to feature their lines anonymously.
This book could not have been produced without the support of those who have contributed illustrations, and I am grateful to all the following: George Barlow (collection), pages 13 (top), 22 (lower); K. Blackham, page 24 (top); Robin Butterell, page 23 (top); Nick and Sue Dodson, page 26; David Enefer, page 15 (lower); Lady Jenny Gretton (collection), page 23 (upper centre); Grimshaw Album, courtesy Simon Townsend and Brian Rogers, pages 7 (centre), 11, 27 (top); Dave Holroyde, pages 15 (top), 17 (centre), 22 (top), 27 (bottom), 30 (top); Peter Johnson, pages 5 (bottom), 21 (bottom), 33, 36 (top), (collection) page 8; Philip Kingston (collection), courtesy Simon Townsend, page 7 (bottom); Neville R. Knight, pages 12 (top), 14 (centre), 17 (top), 28 (centre), 38; Mike Lloyd, page 16 (top); Chris Mansfield, page 28 (top); Austin Moss, page 12 (bottom); Peco Publications & Publicity Ltd, page 20 (bottom); Chris Rennie, pages 18 (centre), 24 (bottom); Adrian Sant, pages 6 (top), 17 (bottom), (collection) page 9 (top); Paul Sharpe, pages 6 (bottom), 10 (both), 14 (top and bottom), 20 (top), 23 (lower left), 35 (lower), 37; Simon Townsend (collection), pages 27 (top), 29 (centre); Peter van Zeller, page 21 (upper right); A. Vaughan, courtesy Paul Conibeare, page 18 (top); J. Waterfield, back cover; Wilde family collection, page 7 (top). Other photographs are by the author or from his collection.

Printed in Malta by Gutenberg Press Limited, Gudja Road,
Tarxien PLA 19, Malta.

Contents

Introduction

The story of miniature railways began with the construction of large model locomotives. Some were built to publicise the work of manufacturers of full-size equipment. Others were built by skilled machinists for their own amusement. It was some time before the first complete miniature railways were constructed with track, rolling stock and all the other paraphernalia needed to create a working railway system, but once the possibilities were widely understood the number of railways steadily increased. Since the last quarter of the nineteenth century they have been a feature of life on country estates and in many private gardens. During the twentieth century they were established at seaside resorts and other tourist centres. They are now to be found throughout the United Kingdom, where there is either an enthusiastic owner or a potential queue of paying passengers.

This book looks at the many different expressions of the miniature railway builder's craft in the United Kingdom. Examples are taken from both private and commercial railways, large and small. The subjects of civil engineering, track construction, locomotives, rolling stock and operating systems are introduced here and can be studied in greater depth elsewhere if readers wish to pursue them.

It is difficult to define the term 'miniature railway'. This book is concerned with those lines that have a miniature railway atmosphere. What is meant by this? Well, part of the answer is that miniature railways give the impression of full-size railways on a reduced scale. Fairground rides that make no attempt to look like or operate as a conventional railway are therefore not included. For the rest of the answer we have to look at the spirit in which the railway is conceived and operated. A miniature railway should have an air of fun about it. Even where it serves a useful purpose a miniature railway is rarely the most obvious answer to a transport problem. Often eccentric, usually a little whimsical, and always small enough for children to relate to them, miniature railways are really an expression of the playful instinct in mankind. Those who take them too seriously run the risk of missing the point. I hope that this little book conveys some of the pleasure that I have had from being involved with them for over thirty years.

Important note

Many of the railways mentioned in this book are strictly private and are identified by the symbol (P). Others are private but have occasional open days (P/OD). Please respect their privacy. If you wish to visit private railways it is best to join the societies mentioned at the end of this book and attend their organised visits.

The 7¹/₄" gauge Brookside Miniature Railway (P) is an example of a miniature railway in a typical modern garden.

All shapes and sizes

Miniature railways come in all shapes and sizes, from a circuit of rails round a suburban garden to express passenger trains on the 13³/₄ mile run across Romney Marsh in Kent. They can be useful for public transport: the Romney line runs regular school trains and the Wells Harbour Railway in Norfolk put the competing bus service out of business. But more often they are built to satisfy someone's personal ambition. Whatever their purpose, the builder's personal preferences (or prejudices) usually guide the design of the railway, and every site is different; therefore no two lines are the same.

An express at full speed on the Romney Hythe and Dymchurch Railway in Kent. This is the most ambitious miniature railway that has ever been built.

The 10¼" gauge Wells Harbour Railway runs from the town of Wells-next-the-Sea in Norfolk to the lifeboat station and Pinewoods Caravan Park at the entrance to the harbour. It was built by Lieutenant Commander Roy Francis and is now the principal method of public transport on this route. The original steam locomotive 'Edmund Hannay' is seen being turned, ready for another journey.

In addition to having the right atmosphere there are some technical features that are common to most miniature railways. First, they can carry human passengers – anything smaller really has to be considered as a model railway. Second, the gauge usually falls within the range 5" to 21" – metric equivalents are given in the table of gauges on page 11 but are never used in practice. Third, their engines are usually smaller versions of full-size counterparts, either real or imaginary. Many enthusiasts would add a fourth definition specifying that they have to be at ground level and include some of the lineside features of a full-size railway. This definition would exclude those tracks that are operated on raised trestles and those that have no junctions or sidings.

In the earliest years attention was focused on locomotives. Tracks usually consisted of merely enough line for demonstrations. When

Model engineers operate trains on elevated tracks, which enable very small gauges to be used but preclude complex layouts. This picture is of the line at Bradford Model Engineering Society, Shipley, Yorkshire.

Sir Arthur Heywood's private garden railway at Duffield Bank with a passenger train hauled by 'Ella'. The open carriages had compartments marked 'First' and 'Second' according to whether there was any padding on the seats. Sir Arthur was an aristocrat of the old school and never charged fares, so perhaps passengers were allocated to the class that reflected their social standing.

J. A. Holder built the 10¼" gauge Broome Railway using equipment from the family's earlier line at Moor Green. Later, most of the equipment was transferred to a house named Keeping, near Beaulieu. The Holder railways were an inspiration to many people because visitors were welcome and because they were the subject of magazine articles, but very few people had the same resources as the Holder family, who were able to employ a full-time engineer.

builders wanted to have a more complete railway system the first garden lines emerged. An early example was at Ardkinglas House in Argyllshire, but very little is known about it. The most famous of the early garden railways was built by Sir Arthur Heywood at Duffield Bank in Derbyshire. This began in 1874 as both a hobby and an experiment to find the smallest railway that could be used for practical purposes such as supplying troops in the field or moving the freight generated by country estates. Because of its purpose and the design of its equipment it was on the borderline between miniature and narrow gauge railways. However, some of the rolling stock – particularly the dining and sleeping carriages – gave it the spirit of a miniature railway. Other railways in private gardens were built simply for pleasure.

The line at Blakesley Hall was another railway built for pleasure but it also had a practical purpose. Guests arriving at the nearby main-line station could summon a special train by telephone. It would arrive at the 15" gauge railway's own platform, driven by the butler. In this view the children on the engine are the owner's son and daughter, James and Ivy Bartholomew.

The development of commercial miniature railways took place fastest in the United States, where the firm of Cagney supplied about 1300 engines, on gauges of $12^5/_8''$, $15''$, $16''$ and $22''$. One of their engines is shown in the historic picture taken at Blakesley Hall (page 7). The Cagney brothers were the suppliers; the locos were actually built by the firms of McGarigle and Herschell-Spillman. Many in the United States were left to rot when a labour protection law was passed that required *all* steam locomotives to have a crew of two people – even if there was room for only one person.

Early commercial miniature railways in the United Kingdom were usually to be found at either exhibitions or seaside resorts. They often consisted of no more than a straight line or circle of track, sometimes with a few features such as a mock tunnel in which the rolling stock could be stored. It is thought that the Cagney engines may have been the inspiration for Henry Greenly and W. J. Bassett-Lowke, who were pioneers of commercial miniature railways in the United Kingdom. Their company, Miniature Railways of Great Britain Ltd, built numerous lines, including one that remains in existence at Rhyl.

It is not only the early lines that had simple designs. Many contemporary miniature railways are also limited to a short length of track, a building in which to keep the train, and somewhere for the passengers to board. Simple construction techniques can be used, although it is usually the case that at least one aspect of the railway is well thought out and competently executed. For example a garden line may be short and have only a four-wheel battery-electric tram to run on it, but the landscaping may consist of imaginative planting to create plenty of interesting viewpoints.

There have been numerous examples of railways that are full of interesting features despite being very short. One such was the Saltwood miniature railway, which was built in 1924 by the Schwab

An early seaside miniature railway of which Henry Greenly was the engineer. Built in 1911 at Rhyl, Denbighshire, Wales, it has survived several transformations and was still running in 2002.

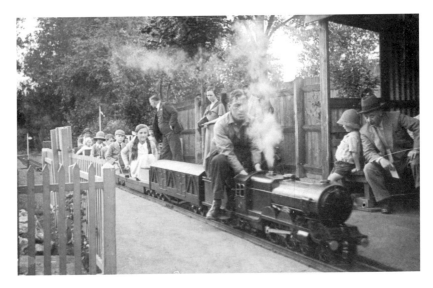

family at Hythe in Kent. It consisted of only 610 feet (186 metres) of track in an oval, but it had its own character and was open to the public regularly until shortly before the death of Alex Schwab in 1987. Another interesting example is the Well Hill Light Railway (P), which runs round a lawn with a single station but has a branch line that climbs to a higher level behind the house; this gives scope to operate two or more trains, so visitors can bring an engine with them. Many operators enjoy sharing their private lines and testing each other's engines on different routes.

The most ambitious miniature railway that has ever been built anywhere in the world is the Romney Hythe and Dymchurch Railway (RH&DR). There have been other impressive lines, including the Surrey Border and Camberley (which closed in 1939),

Above: Although the Saltwood Miniature Railway was very short, it had plenty of character.

Below: Two trains in operation on a small miniature railway. The Well Hill Light Railway (P) makes imaginative use of a confined space.

The Moors Valley Railway shows how busy some commercial miniature railways can be, provided they are in the right location.

The Great Cockcrow Railway at Chertsey in Surrey (P/OD) is the reincarnation of an ambitious 7¹/₄" gauge garden railway built by John Samuel at Walton-on-Thames.

but the RH&DR is still in a class of its own and continues to thrive.

The complexity of miniature railways can manifest in a variety of ways. For example, the RH&DR has a complex inventory of rolling stock, requiring a great deal of equipment simply because it is so long. The Moors Valley Railway in Dorset is much shorter, but it has a complex route system, operating intensive services on track layouts that provide interesting journeys. Some of the most complex of the garden railways have included Sir John Samuel's Greywood Central (now re-created as the Great Cockcrow Railway in Surrey), the Stockholes Farm Miniature Railway in Lincolnshire and the Torry Hill Railway (P). It is possible to give a simple circuit of track the appearance of being quite a complex railway by adding sidings, a good collection of rolling stock, and signals. Nothing in the world of miniature railways is more fun than driving after dark with signal lamps beckoning the train onward. However, the private operator should be wary of adding more complexity than can be coped with. The owner of a large garden railway was once heard to complain that he could no longer push a wagon out to collect fallen autumn leaves because of the signalling and point-locking system that had been installed for him by well-meaning helpers. His railway could now be used only when a team of trained people was available to operate the several signal boxes!

Miniature railway gauges

The gauge of a railway is the distance between the inside faces of the heads of the rails. Ideally, the choice of gauge is dictated by the amount of traffic expected, the sharpness of curves, the length of the journey and other practical considerations.

Locomotives and rolling stock are usually built to run on one particular gauge of track. For example, a $7^1/_4$" gauge locomotive could not operate on a $10^1/_4$" gauge railway. One might expect that this limitation would have led to an early standardisation of gauges, allowing each vehicle to operate on many different railways. In fact the opposite has happened and an astonishing variety of gauges has come into use. The author knows of the following miniature railway gauges in current use in the United Kingdom, and there may be more:

Table of principal British miniature railway gauges

5" (127 mm)	6" (152 mm)	$7^1/_4$" (184 mm)	$8^1/_4$" (209 mm)
9" (228 mm)	$9^1/_2$" (241 mm)	$10^1/_4$" (260 mm)	12" (305 mm)
$12^1/_4$" (311 mm)	15" (381 mm)	20" (508 mm)	21" (533 mm)

The most likely explanation for this diversity is that most miniature railway builders had little thought of their engines and rolling stock running on other railways. Most builders had only their own requirements in mind and they built their railways to a gauge that suited their workshop facilities, their site or the traffic they expected to carry. Surprisingly few gauges have a simple relationship with the full-size standard gauge, which is 4' $8^1/_2$". For

This scene in 1936 on the $10^1/_4$" gauge Keeping Railway shows the driver sitting inside the tender on his locomotive instead of on top as was more usual in $7^1/_4$" gauge locomotives at this time. The 1903 De Dion car in the foreground is now in the National Motor Museum at Beaulieu.

The Romney Hythe and Dymchurch Railway actually has a unique gauge of $15^1/8''$ but is regarded as a 15" gauge line and its locomotives have frequently operated on other railways, as on this occasion in 1984 when 'Samson' worked at the Liverpool International Garden Festival.

example, $1/8$ full-size ($1^1/2$ inches to the foot) has been a popular ratio. It results in a gauge of $7^1/16''$ but the author knows of only one complete railway built to this gauge, by a Mr Copestake about 1896. The $9^1/2''$ gauge was once very popular, and it is very close to a ratio of 1:6 (2 inches to the foot), but it has been overtaken by the $10^1/4''$ gauge, which has very uncertain origins but enables the construction of larger locomotives and carriages.

A serious attempt at standardisation was made by the Society of Model and Experimental Engineers and by the famous designer Henry Greenly, who proposed standards for $7^1/4''$, $9^1/2''$ and 15" gauges, of which those for the $7^1/4''$ gauge probably laid the foundation for one of the most popular sizes of miniature railway today. However, his standards did not attract universal acceptance and he departed from them himself when he built the Romney Hythe and Dymchurch line to $15^1/8''$ gauge instead of 15", as shown on his locomotive drawings and proved by the track gauges. Thankfully, the engineering tolerances of (nominally) 15" gauge railways allow interchanges of engines between most of the lines. One engine that takes regular advantage of this is *Sian*, owned by a group of enthusiasts.

The very earliest miniature railways were seldom built to a gauge much below 15", but by the end of the nineteenth century

Shared ownership of an engine is one way of becoming involved in a miniature railway at a modest cost. On the left of this picture is 'Sian', which is owned by a group of enthusiasts and is seen during a visit to the Windmill Animal Farm Railway, Lancashire.

many model engineers were more confident about the capabilities of small engines, and smaller gauges began to appear. Despite the dictum of Sir Arthur Heywood that 15" is the minimum gauge 'possessing the necessary stability for practical use', there is general agreement that the $7^1/_4$" gauge can be used successfully for miniature railways, both private and public. The first line of this gauge designed for commercial operation was built by Louis Shaw at Ilkeston in 1915, and there are numerous $7^1/_4$" gauge commercial tracks in the United Kingdom today. One that deserves a special mention is the Moors Valley, not only because it is such a well-built and interesting railway but also because it has the distinction of having won a case against HM Customs and Excise. The railway prevailed by proving that despite its small size it provides a genuine transport facility, and therefore VAT does not have to be charged on its tickets.

The smallest gauge in general use at ground level is 5", although $3^1/_2$" and even smaller gauges are possible. These gauges may be

The principal reason why VAT is not chargeable on some miniature railway tickets is that the railway concerned provides a public transport service, as in the case of the $10^1/_4$" gauge line on the island of Mull in the West Highlands of Scotland.

Mixed gauge track enables trains of several different gauges to operate together. This scene shows the Ascot Locomotive Society's original line, which had gauges of 7¹/₄", 5" and 3¹/₂".

Below: In this view of the 12¹/₄" gauge Exmoor Steam Railway at Bratton Fleming in Devon the locomotive was called 'Lorna Doone'. It was built here in 1991 but has since been converted to run elsewhere on 10¹/₄" gauge and is now called 'John Remy

acceptable for private lines, but where the public is carried it is often necessary to provide an extra line of rails on which the passenger carriages can run. Such tracks are referred to as mixed gauge. Some tracks have several different gauges, usually where they are operated by a club, and this requires some complicated points.

Another way to give greater scope for the running of locomotives on different railways is to build them so that they can be converted to run on different gauges. This feature is found on some of the locomotives built by Trevor and Tony Stirland at the Exmoor Steam Railway works in Devon.

A group of 7¹/₄" gauge engines gathered round the turntable at the Weston Park Railway in Staffordshire illustrates the different sizes to be found on the same gauge. The smallest of these engines could be transported in a family estate car; the largest needs a substantial trailer or even a lorry.

This scale model of an early design of locomotive, seen at Donaghadee in Northern Ireland, is very small indeed compared with other engines of the same gauge seen in the previous illustration.

The railway at Cleethorpes in Lincolnshire is now well developed as a leading 15" gauge seaside line, and memories of its rather down-at-heel days are receding.

Gauge does not equal size. There are numerous modern $7^1/4''$ gauge steam engines that are larger than the typical 15" gauge engine of the 1920s, and a scale model of a British standard gauge engine will almost always be smaller than a model of a narrow gauge engine on the same gauge. If there is a current trend in the building of miniature railway locomotives, it is towards building ever larger locomotives for any given gauge. Some of these come close to being narrow gauge engines rather than miniatures and make the true miniatures look very small indeed.

A final word about gauges: when contractors re-laid the miniature railway along the seafront at Cleethorpes in Lincolnshire they were told to make the gauge 15". They knew nothing about railways, and so they carefully measured this dimension between the middle of the rails instead of the inside faces. The result was a unique railway, with a gauge of $14^1/4''$. All the rolling stock had to fit the new gauge, and it was not until a new operating company invested in re-gauging the line to 15" that visiting engines could be accommodated.

15

The 7¼" gauge Woodside Light Railway (P) has been built on the side of a steep hill, proving that even very difficult terrain can accommodate a miniature railway.

Civil engineering, track and buildings

If the traffic to be carried by a miniature railway consists merely of family and friends, and the site is the back garden of the family home, the civil engineering may be quite simple. But the degree of slope in a garden may be surprisingly large, and even these domestic lines sometimes need quite extensive civil engineering. The builder may even choose to create artificial hills, valleys, lakes and waterfalls to provide an excuse for tunnels, embankments and bridges, all of which add interest. Reduced costs of hiring diesel hydraulic excavators and their ready availability have tempted many people to undertake ambitious landscaping.

If the traffic consists of paying customers and the line is set up to make a profit the builder will usually try to minimise the investment in civil engineering, but not if this results in excessive gradients. The

The Chaldon Light Railway (P) occupies a garden that includes a worked-out quarry, a corner of which is crossed by a high-level bridge. Notice how well hidden the railway is; the only time you would know it is there is when a train steams past!

16

This view shows a tunnel under construction on the 10¹/₄" gauge Audley End Railway in Essex using the 'cut and cover' method. First a cutting is dug and the railway laid, then the tunnel itself is built and finally the tunnel is covered over with soil. This method is much cheaper than boring a tunnel underground.

factor that places the greatest limitation on the number of passengers a train can carry is not the gauge; it is the ruling gradient, that is, the steepest gradient on the line. This is partly because of the tractive effort required to haul a train uphill and partly because miniature railway engines can suffer from a lack of adhesion, especially when the rails are wet or greasy. In these circumstances passengers may see the wheels spinning (known as slipping) because the engine has lost its grip. This can be remedied by an application of dry sand to give the engine additional adhesion.

For lines that are several miles long the easiest type of route is a disused

This private railway makes stunning use of a spectacularly beautiful site and includes a tunnel that harks back to the architectural extravagance of the late eighteenth and early nineteenth centuries. The castellated tower is a modern folly, in which a professional hermit can be incarcerated on special occasions to wave at the trains passing below.

Garratt locomotive 'Norfolk Hero' at Wells-next-the-Sea in Norfolk having brought in a train from Walsingham on the longest 10¹/₄" gauge railway in the world.

17

The 15" gauge express trains of the Bure Valley Railway in Norfolk share their trackbed with cyclists and walkers, thus enabling a single route to accommodate three highly sustainable forms of transport.

trackbed from a previous railway. The Wells and Walsingham Light Railway in Norfolk uses this type of site for a 4 mile journey through delightful countryside to the pilgrimage town of Walsingham. In the same county the Bure Valley Railway runs on the trackbed of the old East Norfolk Railway between Wroxham and Aylsham and shares its route very successfully with both pedestrians and cyclists. It is said that in 1948 the pioneer railway preservationist L. T. C. Rolt considered converting the world-famous Tal-y-llyn Railway to $10^1/4$" gauge. Even the most avid miniature railway enthusiast must be glad that this did not occur.

Miniature railway track consists of five major components:
* A **roadbed**, which must include a drainage system – this is of crucial importance. Drainage may require pipes but is often accomplished using soakaways.
* **Ballast**, which consists of crushed stone underneath and

Above: *This specially commissioned picture shows different stages of construction on the 5" gauge Corris Hill Railway (P). In this case there is a foundation of hardcore, a layer of black geotextile membrane, the ballast and finally the track itself. On the smaller gauges it is usual to provide edging strips of treated timber or, as in this case, concrete path-edgers.*

Right: *Laying new sidings on the 15" gauge Perrygrove Railway in the Royal Forest of Dean, Gloucestershire. The platelayers are using a hydraulic tool called a Jim Crow to bend the steel rails. On the ground in front of them is a traditional Jim Crow – a fearsome beast that weighs well over a hundredweight and has to be screwed by hand using a steel crowbar that is 6 feet long.*

The 7¹/₄" gauge Porters Hill Railway (P) had been running for twenty-five years when this picture was taken in 2000, and its tracks have the correct appearance for a charming rural byway.

around the sides of the sleepers. This holds the track in place, provides a resilient base that avoids too hard a ride for the trains, and permits drainage. Many modern railways separate the ballast from the underlying ground with a geotextile membrane – a sheet of special polymer – that stops the ballast being mixed into the soil. The best ballast consists of sharp-edged stones, usually crushed limestone, that interlock with each other. Some railways use flints, sea shingle or other stones with rounded edges, but these often perform very badly.

* **Sleepers** hold the rails to the gauge and transmit the load of the train to the ballast. They may be made of good-quality treated softwood, hardwood, concrete, steel, plastic (on small gauges) or other materials.
* The **rails** of a miniature railway are made from metals such as manganese steel (the same material that is used on full-size railways), mild steel or an aluminium alloy. They have to be the correct shape and size for the loads they are to carry and the profiles of the wheels that are to run on them. It is important that the rails are carefully bent all the way round on curves. If this is not done, kinks, called dog-legs, will develop at the joints.
* The **fixings** consist of devices that hold the rails to the sleepers and fishplates with bolts connecting adjoining rails together.

Below: An example of a private 15" gauge garden railway where the buildings – in this case the engine shed – have been carefully designed to suit their surroundings. Also note the light rail, sharp curves and restricted clearances. These features enable the railway to stay on the perimeter of the garden, screened from view by careful planting.

That is the theory, and for commercial lines it should also be the practice. But many private miniature railways manage without any immediately discernible drainage system, with ballast made up of various sorts of stone chippings or brick hardcore, with sleepers made from different sections of wood, many types of rail, much of which was not designed for the purpose, and with fixings from the box of spare screws. Some of these railways have a particularly attractive character and have operated for many years without any accidents.

The signal box on the railway at Audley End is a miniature replica of the real thing – complete with miniature signalman!

The buildings of the 7¹/₄" gauge Beer Heights Light Railway at Pecorama in Beer, Devon, are small rather than miniature and suit the trains well.

In the author's view, some of the most aesthetically pleasing miniature railways achieve their good looks because of the suitability and attractiveness of their buildings. It is very tempting for a miniature railway operator to save money by storing trains in the security of a steel shipping container or a second-hand concrete garage building, but good architecture enhances a miniature railway and can be of as much interest as the trains.

Some miniature railways provide miniature buildings to complement the scale-size of the trains, as at Audley End in Essex, but others use full-size buildings which with careful design can avoid being grotesque when the miniature trains are set against them, as at the Beer Heights Light Railway in Devon.

Locomotives

The two most important distinctions between miniature locomotive designs are motive power and style.

The most common types of motive power are electricity (from batteries or a low-voltage feed to the track), internal combustion (petrol, gas or diesel) and steam (raised from a coal, oil or propane gas fire). A hybrid type is the 'pretender' – an engine that looks from the outside like a steam locomotive but is actually powered by electricity or internal combustion. Examples of all these forms can be seen when visiting commercial miniature railways. On some railways a variety of types can be seen, for example on the Ravenglass and Eskdale in Cumbria, which has a battery-electric shunting locomotive, and main-line engines powered by diesel and steam.

Above left: The simplest motive power unit that any miniature railway can have is a battery-electric tram such as this example, which children are allowed to drive on the Well Hill Railway (P).

Above right: One of the locomotives on the Blakesley Hall Line was 'Blacolvesley', an example of a locomotive that looks as though it is steam-powered but in fact has an internal combustion engine. It has been preserved by Dr Bob Tebb and is believed to be the world's oldest surviving internal combustion railway locomotive.

A line-up of different types of locomotive on the 15" gauge Ravenglass and Eskdale Railway in Cumbria, including (left to right) battery-electric, diesel and steam examples.

The historic 9" gauge Torry Hill Railway (P) has a remarkable collection of vintage miniature locomotives, which operate over an extensive route including a viaduct built of miniature bricks and a long tunnel. The railway suffered enormous damage in the great storm of 1987 and the operator (the grandson of the founder) had to spend over seven years rebuilding it.

When Henry Greenly drew the plans for a 'Pacific' type locomotive in 1924 he knew that his customers wanted something that had the appearance of the crack express engines of the London and North Eastern Railway. The result was a truly original design. One of the three engines of this type is 'Green Goddess', seen here with George Barlow BEM, her regular driver for thirty-one years.

Turning to style, the traditional miniature steam locomotive is either a scaled-down version of a full-size example, such as those on the Torry Hill Railway (P), or is at least reminiscent of a full-size prototype, for example *Green Goddess* on the Romney Hythe and Dymchurch Railway. For many years the prototypes for miniature railway engines were almost always standard gauge examples. However, an exact scale model was found to be insufficiently robust for heavy use. Designers therefore aimed for the appearance of main-line locomotives of their era, but with subtle changes that enabled them to perform well. Examples include Henry Greenly's *Little Giant* of 1905 and *River Esk* of 1923, and later designs, such as David Curwen's excellent machines, which have been stalwarts at the Stapleford, Leicestershire, (P/OD) and Audley End railways, amongst others. When diesels arrived on the scene the same principle was followed, so that the general appearance of the full-size machine was achieved but with the miniature version often powered by a petrol engine and with a different form of transmission from the original. An example of such a locomotive is shown in the picture of the Audley End signal box (page 20).

Another approach has been to use narrow gauge railways for prototypes. Some very large and complex locomotives have

The original 'Little Giant' of 1905 has been restored to working order and is seen here at Dalegarth on a visit to the Ravenglass and Eskdale Railway.

Right: This 4-4-2 'Atlantic' type locomotive is one of several built by David Curwen, often with an American appearance. They are extremely reliable engines on several busy railways. This example is 'John of Gaunt', seen on the Stapleford Miniature Railway in Leicestershire (P/OD) under the command of the late Lord Gretton.

Above: This 7¼" gauge miniature of the South African 'Garratt' type locomotive represents miniature railway superpower. Few railways could provide enough passenger coaches to test its full hauling capacity. No. 5928, 'Mount Kilimanjaro', was built by Coleby/Simkins in 1973 and is seen on the Weston Park Railway in 2000.

Right: Even an experienced driver welcomes some advice before taking the controls of something as large and complex as a Garratt locomotive.

Above: *Looking over the shoulder of the driver on this private 7¹/₄" gauge line in Herefordshire, we are reminded that as well as controlling his steam locomotive's speed and looking out for signals he also has to maintain the fire and the boiler water level – a job for two on anything other than a miniature railway.*

resulted, for instance the South African Garratt types.

There has been a growth in the popularity of locomotives that are not based on any prototype, and some of these test the boundaries of the miniature railway definition because they are more like very small narrow gauge locomotives than miniatures. A famous example of 7¹/₄" gauge is the *Tinkerbell* type, which enables its driver to sit in a proper cab space. Since this first appeared in 1968 there have been numerous other examples.

An important feature of most miniature steam engines is that the driver also has to be the fireman and therefore has to do the work of two people; three if the role of a guard is also required. Driving a miniature steam train safely is not a sinecure.

Newcomers to the world of miniature railways are well advised to begin with a locomotive that they can run on other people's railways. The easiest way of achieving this is to purchase a brand-new machine from a reputable supplier.

This view of a small steam locomotive shows the sort of machine that is available off the shelf, or at least within a short period, from established manufacturers. The example shown is 5" gauge.

The skilled engineer with a small workshop can build miniature locomotives and rolling stock from raw materials – which can even include scraps and off-cuts from industrial workshops. Some people can achieve good results with nothing more than a lathe, a bench drill and a bench grinder. However, a milling machine and a powered saw are useful additions.

The 10¼" gauge 'Scots Guardsman' is winched into a van after visiting the Wilderness Railway (P) during a grand tour of the United Kingdom. This locomotive is usually based on the South Downs Light Railway at the Pulborough Garden Centre in West Sussex. The tank engine in the foreground was built at the Exmoor Steam Railway in 1989. Originally 7¼" gauge, it was rebuilt for 12¼", then re-gauged again for this line.

Engines are also available second-hand through classified advertisements in the relevant magazines and society journals. Many people build their own locomotives, sometimes starting with a simple battery-electric tram that can be completed within a year using bought-in components and hand tools. At the other end of the scale is a complicated steam locomotive that may take seven or even twelve years of spare-time work to complete. As a guide, an experienced engineer may take about 1600 hours to build a simple medium-sized steam engine and double that to build a detailed scale model. The author knows of one 7¼" gauge locomotive that took its builder 7000 hours to construct.

A 5" or small 7¼" gauge engine can be lifted into an estate car for transport. Larger machines need a trailer or a van. At the top end of the scale, a large 15" gauge locomotive will need a heavy goods vehicle to transport it and a journey using this form of transport usually costs several hundred pounds with the possible additional cost of a crane to load and unload it at each end of its journey.

In early 2002 a new electric locomotive for a small gauge cost from about £1000, rising to £60,000 for a powerful 15" gauge diesel. A small steam locomotive for private use could be purchased for about £6000 and one suitable for commercial operation was priced at about

The 2-6-4T 'Mark Timothy' leaves the Perrygrove Railway after a visit in 2001, whilst the resident 0-6-0T 'Spirit of Adventure' raises steam on the engine-shed road. There is a loading dock at this location, but on this occasion the departing locomotive was lifted on to the lorry by an on-board hydraulic crane.

£13,000. At the upper end of the scale, the cost of a large 15" gauge steam locomotive could easily exceed £100,000, and a fast express engine like those on the RH&DR would be unlikely to cost less than a quarter of a million pounds. VAT would usually have to be added to these prices.

Second-hand prices for locomotives vary enormously. Machines are advertised for sale in the journals of the $7^1/4$" Gauge Society and Narrow Gauge Railway Society, in several magazines and on the internet.

Simple battery-electric locomotives, similar to this sort of design, can be purchased from several manufacturers. They have no exhaust emissions and are therefore useful for builders who wish to follow the example shown, where the railroad runs through the middle of the house!

The 10¹/₄" gauge railway built by Sir John Holder in the 1890s at his home, Pitmaston, in the Birmingham suburb of Moor Green, used miniature goods wagons to carry passengers.

Rolling stock

Miniature railway rolling stock, like locomotives, can be replicas of full-size examples, reminiscent of them, or completely individual.

Passenger vehicles on some of the early lines were models of full-size vehicles, including goods trucks, as seen in the picture of the 10¹/₄" gauge Pitmaston Moor Green Railway. It is possible to buy miniature versions of full-size passenger coaches for 7¹/₄" gauge, and these do give quite a comfortable ride. The advantage of replica vehicles is that when passengers are not being carried the train can give a very good impression of a full-size version. The disadvantage is that when passengers are carried the dichotomy between vehicle and passengers can be rather too obvious for comfort.

The simplest types of miniature railway carriages are the 'sit-astride' and the 'toastrack'. The first is most popular on smaller

Modern passenger coaches that are replicas of full-size examples give a comfortable ride and are often equipped with continuous brakes. These examples are seen on the 7¹/₄" gauge Stockholes Farm Railway near Belton in Lincolnshire (P/OD).

On a sit-astride coach the passengers are seated on a bench, resembling a small vaulting horse, that runs the length of the vehicle. These examples are of 7¹/₄" gauge, on the railway at Brookside Garden Centre, Poynton, Cheshire. The engine is a 0-4-2T named 'Jean', built by Exmoor Steam Railway in 2000.

gauges and was developed from the designs used for the elevated tracks at model engineering societies. It has the virtues of simple construction and good stability. Its disadvantages are that there may not be anything to keep children's legs within the carriage, the visual appearance has little to commend it, and ladies wearing skirts find it awkward to say the least. The toastrack carriage does at least allow the passengers to sit on conventional seats and is a very practical type with many years' safe operation to its credit. Unfortunately, it has become associated with fairground rides, not least because traditional roller-coaster trains are of this type. A solution to these problems is the sit-astride design with sides, examples of which can be seen in the picture of the Moors Valley Railway (page 10).

The British climate makes enclosed carriages popular on many miniature railways. On 7¹/₄" gauge they were first introduced on the Hilton Valley Railway and they have since been adopted by several other lines. However, careful design is necessary

Above: 'Toastrack' coaches are given this name because of their appearance. There are various permutations on the theme; these examples were at the Belle Vue Railway in Manchester. Whilst the railway is long gone, the locomotive, 'Joan', could still be seen at Rhyl in 2002.

Right: The earliest covered coaches on the 7¹/₄" gauge were those provided for the Hilton Valley Railway. The original line closed in 1979 but many of the coaches now operate on other railways, including this private line where there is a particularly fine station building.

Another covered coach on the 7¹/₄" gauge. The author has ridden in this vehicle and can testify that it seemed fairly stable. One of the problems of such coaches is their incongruity when hauled by a 'miniature' locomotive.

if such vehicles are to be sufficiently stable. On one occasion the author was one of the passengers in a 7¹/₄" gauge enclosed carriage that derailed and then tipped over on to its side – fortunately without causing any injuries. On 10¹/₄" gauge, enclosed carriages can be more stable.

Other miniature railway operators have elected to develop their own individual designs that fit neatly into the overall ambience of their surroundings. The earliest examples were those of Sir Arthur Heywood, but many other people have adopted a similar approach.

Freight vehicles can be categorised as miniature or utility. The

The 10¹/₄" gauge Surrey Border and Camberley Railway had a very short existence but its story is fascinating and is very well told in a book by Mitchell, Townsend and Shelmerdine (see 'Further reading'). The railway's closed carriages are seen in this view of the main terminus.

Many people build home-made coaches to their own designs, such as these examples on the Woodbine Cottage Garden Railway.

The coaches in this picture were designed by Trevor and Tony Stirland of the Exmoor Steam Railway for the 15" gauge Markeaton Park Railway at Derby. This partnership also built the engine 'Markeaton Lady'.

former are found most frequently on smaller gauges – typically up to $10^1/4''$ (although there are a few larger examples) – and their purpose is to model a full-size freight train.

Utility freight vehicles are more often found on lines that lie on the border between miniature and narrow gauge. On the Ravenglass and Eskdale, up to about 20,000 tons of granite were carried each year from Beckfoot quarry in purpose-made steel wagons, a few of which still survive. On the RH&DR, shingle ballast used to be carried at night when the passenger service had finished. The

The 15" gauge railway at Eaton Hall (P) was constructed for the carriage of freight. This view shows the exchange sidings at Balderton in 1896, where coal was loaded. There is no longer any trace of the railway at this location.

These wagons are used for construction and maintenance work on the 7¹⁄₄" gauge Porters Hill Railway (P).

Shillingstone Light Railway's reason for existence was to serve a pig farm, where a high water-table frequently resulted in tractors becoming bogged down. It was only 10¹⁄₄" gauge, but it had wagons for carrying feed, manure, whey and piglets. Unfortunately, no pictures survive to show the piglet wagon in use.

Most miniature railways have some wagons that are designed for maintenance and other specialised purposes. The simplest are open wagons for carrying ballast, and most railways have a few of these. Other examples are bogie wagons for carrying timber and other long loads, spraying wagons for weed control, coal and oil wagons for locomotive fuel, and general-purpose covered wagons known as box vans.

Some miniature railway vehicles are built just for fun; for example James Waterfield's recreation of Sir Arthur Heywood's 'bit of Victorian whimsy' (as the builder describes it): the Duffield Bank

This view shows part of the goods-wagon fleet on the Perrygrove Railway. The wagons in the foreground were built by Sir Arthur Heywood and are rare survivors. Those in the background include some that were in industrial use and others that have been built for this line.

In 2000 the Duffield Bank dining carriage visited Ravenglass together with 'Ursula' and is seen here at Muncaster Mill station during a dinner party at which the guests included Sir Peter and Lady Jackie Heywood. Sir Peter is the great-grandson of Sir Arthur Heywood.

Dining Carriage. This is complete with an antique Rippingille oil stove, Victorian silver cutlery, specially engraved glassware and even a wind-up gramophone playing period music. It looks particularly stylish alongside the same builder's recreation of Sir Arthur Heywood's last locomotive, *Ursula*, which was built originally for the Duke of Westminster's 15" gauge railway at Eaton Hall (P).

Of all miniature railway vehicles, the one that was probably most fun for children was the unique sleeping carriage at Duffield Bank. This had four narrow berths and was reputed to have occasionally carried youthful passengers through the night on a continuous route through the woods. How well did they sleep, one wonders, and when morning came did they take their breakfast in the Dining Carriage?

One feature of miniature railway rolling stock that is of endless amusement when vehicles travel away from their home base is the

incompatibility of drawgear (couplings) and braking systems. The disparity of gauges is nothing compared to the chaos that reigns over coupling and brake design. Passengers have sometimes been left behind by their engine when incompatible couplings have parted company halfway through a journey. The miniature railway tradition calls for those who are marooned in this way to disembark and push their carriages onward to the next station, where their engine will (probably) be waiting for them whilst the driver utilises the enforced delay to enjoy a well-earned mug of tea.

The Duffield Bank dining carriage is a replica but it includes a Rippingille oil stove just like the original.

Operating systems and signalling

Railways are no more inherently safe than any other method of transport, and experience has sadly shown that serious and even fatal accidents are possible on miniature railways. The excellent safety record of most modern railways, including miniature lines, results from the use of operating systems to prevent situations arising in which accidents might happen. Most systems are based on a rule book that lays down safe procedures, and even the most basic line should provide a set of written rules for its staff to follow.

Even a good operating system is ineffective if trains cannot easily be stopped, and on some miniature railways a continuous brake is used, operated usually by air, either above or below atmospheric pressure (respectively the compressed air and the vacuum systems). The aim is that either driver or guard can apply a brake throughout the train and also that the brake will apply automatically if the train becomes divided.

As soon as there is the possibility of two trains occupying a section of track simultaneously there is the need for a system to prevent collisions. In the early days of railways a set period of time had to elapse between trains. However, a train that had stopped unexpectedly could be hit from behind by the following train, and so the absolute block method of working was introduced. This divides railways into defined sections of track, and procedures are then devised to ensure that only one train can enter each section at a time.

On single tracks the simplest system is to have a single physical item provided for each section and a rule that no vehicle is allowed to go into that section unless the person in charge is in possession of the item. The items, known as staffs, tablets or tokens, are referred to collectively as staffs in this chapter. Passengers can often see such an

Exchanging the staff – the driver of the left-hand train cannot proceed on the single line ahead until he has the staff in his possession. This picture was taken on the 12¹/₄" gauge Fairbourne and Barmouth Railway in North Wales.

The interior of the Kingsmere East signal box on the Moors Valley Railway. This has a traditional lever frame for operating points and semaphore signals. On the shelf in front of the signalman is a full set of traditional instruments that ensure a safe distance between trains. There is also an illuminated track plan of the station.

item being exchanged as their train enters and leaves sections of track. If more than one train needs to follow another in the same direction a staff and ticket system can be used. The driver of the first train is shown the staff, which shows that there is no risk of meeting another train coming from the opposite direction, and is given a paper ticket authorising him to set off. When the first train has reached the end of the section a message is sent back and the next train follows, the process being repeated as often as necessary until the final train in that direction carries the staff itself. Alternatively, two electrically interlocked machines can be provided, one at each end of the section, so that once a staff has been issued by one of the machines no further staffs can be issued from either machine until the first one has been replaced.

On double tracks, where trains usually proceed in one direction only on each line, the absolute block system divides the line into sections and trains are controlled so that no train can enter a block section whilst it is still occupied by a preceding train.

Miniature semaphore signals are amongst a range of products that are now available ready-made. This example is on the Oldown miniature railway in Gloucestershire.

Like most artefacts on miniature railways, colour light signals can be either accurate scale models of full-size devices or home-made versions designed to do the job reliably in the simplest possible way, as in this example on a private 7¼" gauge garden railway in the Lake District.

It is easy to imagine the dangerous chaos that could result where a complex track layout requires equally complicated signalling, for example in the approach to the main station of the Great Cockcrow Railway. Safe operation is assured in such locations by interlocking the various points and signals to ensure that conflicting movements are prevented.

Fixed signals are usually the most visible part of any operating system. Their purpose is to convey instructions to the driver of a train and to indicate the route that has been set up at points. Fixed lineside signals began to appear in the 1830s, and from about 1841 the traditional British signal of the semaphore type began to appear. During the last half of the twentieth century these were replaced on most full-size railways by colour lights, which are easier for drivers to see (particularly in bad weather and at night), cheaper to provide and maintain, and easier to control by automatic systems. These advantages have led to their use on many miniature railways.

Two vitally important features of signalling systems are that they should fail to a safe condition – which means they should show a danger signal when things go wrong – and that there should be interlocking controls so that it is impossible for the operator to set up conflicting train movements that could result in a collision. Effective interlocking systems require signalling controls to be concentrated together and the result is the traditional cabin, or signal box, which is an attractive feature on many miniature railways.

A driver can still ignore or miss a signal and thereby cause an accident. The operator who wishes to prevent this happening needs

The 12" gauge Ruislip Lido Miniature Railway is one line that offers Londoners an opportunity to enjoy the miniature railway scene close to home. Train control is carried out very professionally here.

to install some form of automatic train control. Such a feature is seldom seen on miniature railways.

All these systems rely on certainty that a section of track is clear before a train enters it. Tail markers or electric track circuits are therefore used to show that when a train leaves a section no vehicle has been left behind.

As soon as there is more than one location from which control is exercised on a railway it is necessary to have a system of communication. This can take the form of a traditional electric telegraph, bells that are operated electrically, telephones or radio. Many railways use one of these systems and a few use combinations.

One of the most interesting operating systems is to be seen on the Ravenglass and Eskdale line – known as the Ratty. At Ravenglass station there is a traditional signal box and a small forest of semaphore signals, but the remainder of the railway is under a system of radio control. On a busy day there may be as many as five trains out on the line at a time, crossing each other at Muncaster Mill siding and the passing loops at Miteside, Irton Road and Fisherground. It is fascinating to eavesdrop on the radio and listen to the steady voice of the railway's controller as he calmly ensures the safety of miniature trains that are carrying the same number of passengers as several large airliners. The Ratty was a pioneer of radio control on British railways and similar systems are now used on other miniature lines, including the Bure Valley and, in London, the Ruislip Lido Railway.

Miniature railways with sound operating systems can be controlled safely by children, under adult supervision, as happens at the Downs Light Railway (P/OD). Of course, it is helpful that this railway's adult supervisors include James Boyd, who was writing books on narrow gauge railways when most people thought them mere anachronisms, and Patrick Keef, whose family firm is a leading supplier of industrial and leisure narrow gauge railway equipment.

The 9½" gauge Downs Light Railway (P/OD) is in the grounds of a prep school. The line is over seventy-five years old and is famous because it is operated by the schoolchildren. Its story is told in the book 'Don't Stand Up in the Tunnel!' (see 'Further reading'). This picture shows some of the staff in 2001. The best way of seeing this remarkable institution is to join one of the societies that arrange visits to such places.

Places to visit

The gazetteer that follows lists over 200 miniature railways that were expected to be open to the public in Britain during 2002. There are difficulties in providing complete information about all of them because every year some lines are extended and others are truncated, new lines are opened and old ones closed, often without warning. Long-established and successful lines can suddenly lose their sites. For example, the superb 15" gauge line in Sutton Park at Sutton Coldfield was forced to close in 1962 because the local authority refused to renew the lease of its land even though it carried about 100,000 passengers a year. Many locomotives are peripatetic and the location of a particular machine can vary. The author's own railway once had a visit from a young enthusiast who had chased the engine *Ursula* from Cleethorpes in Lincolnshire to Aylsham in Norfolk, always being one step behind until he ran it to earth in the Perrygrove engine shed.

This constant activity is one of the fascinating features of miniature railways – you can never be sure what you will find on any visit. But it does mean that the gazetteer does not attempt to provide every detail about the railways.

The summer season – particularly during school holidays – is when most commercial miniature railways operate. A considerable number operate every weekend throughout most of the year. Some are also open at Christmas for Santa Specials and many private operators look forward to winter running.

A word of caution is needed: railways sometimes have notable collections of locomotives but, frustratingly, the only ones you will be able to see during your visit are those pulling the trains whilst the others are locked away in a shed somewhere. This can happen even if the railway's publicity material entices you with a description of all its engines.

To obtain up-to-date information about miniature railways you can subscribe to the Narrow Gauge Railway Society or the Branch Line Society – see 'Societies, clubs and magazines'. The membership fees of these societies are by tradition kept at very reasonable rates. Two guides are published regularly: the *ABC of Miniature Railways* is a biennial publication and is very well illustrated; *Minor Railways* is an annual list – see 'Further reading'.

Whichever source you use, I do hope that you will enjoy visiting miniature railways,

Many miniature railway operators retire to their workshops in winter but some hardy individuals look forward to the challenge of operating throughout the year. For children it can be a magical experience to ride on a tiny steam train through a snowy wood.

whether your interest is in their history, locomotives, or one of their many other aspects. In my own case I have enjoyed visits to many different lines, but one visit in particular stands out.

The 7¹/₄" gauge Hilton Valley Railway in Shropshire ran beside a brook at the bottom of the garden of a large private house. On summer Sundays it was open to the public. Rides were priced at one shilling (5 new pence) for 'all classes' and the proceeds went to charity. My visit was over thirty years ago, and the railway closed in 1979. But it lives in my memory because of the friendly conversation I had with the owner, Michael Lloyd, the pleasure of a ride through beautiful surroundings on good track in comfortable carriages, and the way I was given the freedom to wander through the engine sheds. That visit has stayed in my mind whilst other events of my life – theoretically more important – have long been forgotten. On winter evenings I can pick up the illustrated guidebook that I bought at the Hilton Valley Railway, and out of its pages pour the brook and the birdsong and the whistles of the little trains with their friendly crews, all from that one far-off summer's day. Days like this, and railways like the Hilton Valley, have brought me great enjoyment and I hope that those who read this book will enjoy similar days themselves.

Miniature railway memories … Locomotive 'Michael Charles Lloyd MBE' takes its train down the valley beside the bubbling brook and passes the first daffodils of the last springtime before closure of the Hilton Valley Railway.

Gazetteer

This gazetteer is based on the work of Dave Holroyde of the Narrow Gauge Railway Society, and *Minor Railways* published by Peter Scott (see 'Further reading' and 'Societies, clubs and magazines'). Please note the following:

Addresses are of the railways themselves. Postal addresses of their operators may be different.

Websites seem to come and go even more quickly than miniature railways and it is very hard to know which ones are approved by the railways they cover. They have therefore been omitted from the gazetteer.

Telephone numbers are not included because many railways do not themselves publish an official number and changes are frequent. The local Tourist Information Centre may be able to help.

Operating dates and times – regrettably, it is impractical to include this information because of the space it would take up and the speed with which it would go out of date. Very few miniature railways operate every day, even during the summer, so do check before setting out if possible.

Etiquette. If a site is not open it is very bad form to try to get in. This applies particularly to sites marked P/OD on days when the railway is closed. It is extremely bad manners to turn up, take pictures, talk to the operator, and leave without buying a ticket. Please do not get cross with the operator if the engine breaks down – he or she is more unhappy about it than you are.

A tip: miniature railway ephemera is collectable. If there are picture postcards or a guidebook on sale, or you come across old miniature railway items in good condition at a reasonable price, snap them up and keep them safe.

Caveat: the information in this gazetteer was checked in May 2002. If you decide to use the information for any purpose this will be at your own risk and no liability will be accepted by the author or publisher for any consequences, whether direct or indirect, including any that result from any error, omission or misrepresentation.

NOTES

All gauges are given in inches.

*   Steam locomotives are available but are not necessarily used on all working days.
CT   Club track. Operated occasionally and not always when the site is open for other facilities. Access may be restricted when the railway is not operating.
MES   Model Engineering Society.
MR   Miniature railway.
P/OD   Private with open days. No access whatsoever unless the railway is advertised as open.
SoME   Society of Model Engineers.
UC   Under construction at the time of going to press.

Unscheduled repairs may be needed on even the best-run railways. Here the front pony truck of a large 15" gauge engine receives attention – the author can testify that it was back in place in time for the locomotive to resume its duties.

Bedfordshire

	$7^1/_4$	Fancott Miniature Railway, Fancott, near Toddington
*	$7^1/_4$	Summerfields Fruit Farm, Haynes, near Bedford (CT)
	20	Woburn Safari Park

Berkshire

*	$7^1/_4$	Ascot Locomotive Society – relocating to new site (CT)
*	$10^1/_4$	Beale Park, Pangbourne
*	$7^1/_4$	Pinewood Leisure Centre, Crowthorne (CT)
*	$7^1/_4$	Reading SoME, Prospect Park, Reading (CT)

Bristol

*	$7^1/_4$	Ashton Court Park, Bristol (CT)

Buckinghamshire

	$7^1/_4$	Bekonscot Light Railway, Beaconsfield
*	$7^1/_4$	Buckinghamshire Railway Centre, Quainton Road Station (CT)
	15	Gulliver's Land, Milton Keynes
*	$7^1/_4$	Kingfisher Country Club, Milton Keynes (CT)
*	$7^1/_4$	Willen MR, Milton Keynes

Cambridgeshire

*	$7^1/_4$	Dunham Woods Light Railway, March
*	$10^1/_4$	Ferry Meadows MR, Nene Valley Park, Peterborough
*	$7^1/_4$	Grantchester Woodland Railway, Newnham, Cambridge (CT)
*	$7^1/_4$	Mereside Farm, Ramsey (CT)
*	$7^1/_4$	Thorpe Hall, Peterborough (CT)

Cheshire

*	$7^1/_4$	Brookside Garden Centre, Poynton
*	$7^1/_4$	Dragon MR, Marple
*	$7^1/_4$	Grosvenor Park MR, Chester
	15	Gulliver's World, Warrington
*	$7^1/_4$	Halton MR, Town Park, Halton, Runcorn
	$7^1/_4$	Hills Garden Centre, Allostock, Holmes Chapel (UC)
*	$7^1/_4$	Railway Age, Crewe
*	$7^1/_4$	Sandway, Cuddington (CT)
*	$7^1/_4$	Royden Park, Frankby, Wirral (CT)

Cornwall

*	$7^1/_4$	Dobwalls Family Adventure Park
	$7^1/_4$	Little Western Railway, Trenance Leisure Park, Newquay
*	15	Lappa Valley Steam Railway, Benny Mill, St Newlyn East (also $7^1/_4$, $10^1/_4$)
	15	Paradise Park, Hayle
*	15	Brocklands Adventure Park, Kilkhampton
	$7^1/_4$	Old MacDonald's Farm, Porthcothan Bay

Cumbria

	$7^1/_4$	Lowther Parklands, Hackthorpe
*	$7^1/_4$	Millerbeck Railway, Staveley (P/OD)
*	$7^1/_4$	Port Haverigg Holiday Village, Millom
*	15	Ravenglass and Eskdale Railway
	$7^1/_4$	Solway Holiday Park, Silloth (UC)
	$7^1/_4$	South Lakes Wild Animal Park, Dalton-in-Furness
*	$7^1/_4$	Upperby Park, Carlisle (CT)

Derbyshire

	15	American Adventure World, Ilkeston
	$9^1/_2$	Hall Leys Park, Matlock
*	$7^1/_4$	Manor Park MR, Glossop
*	15	Markeaton Park, Derby
	$12^1/_4$	Pavilion Gardens, Buxton
	$10^1/_4$	Queen's Park, Chesterfield
*	$7^1/_4$	St Peter's School, Hady, Chesterfield (CT)

Devon

*	$7^1/_4$	Beer Heights Light Railway, Pecorama, Beer

*	$10\frac{1}{4}$	Bickington Steam Railway, Trago Mills, Liverton, Newton Abbot
*	$7\frac{1}{4}$	Buckfastleigh MR, South Devon Railway, Buckfastleigh (CT)
	15	Combe Martin Wildlife Park
	$7\frac{1}{4}$	Devon Railway Centre, Bickleigh, Tiverton
*	$12\frac{1}{4}$	Exmoor Steam Railway, Bratton Fleming
	$10\frac{1}{4}$	Exmouth Express, Exmouth
*	$7\frac{1}{4}$	Goodwin Park, Plymouth (CT)
*	$7\frac{1}{4}$	Gorse Blossom MR, Liverton, Newton Abbot (uncertain)
*	$10\frac{1}{4}$	Paignton Environmental Park
*	15	Powderham Castle, Exeter

Dorset

*	$7\frac{1}{4}$	Budmouth Technology College, Weymouth (CT)
*	$7\frac{1}{4}$	Moors Valley Railway, Ashley Heath, Ringwood
	$10\frac{1}{4}$	Poole Park MR, Poole
*	$7\frac{1}{4}$	Purbeck School, Wareham (CT)
	$10\frac{1}{4}$	Weymouth Bay MR, Lodmoor, Weymouth

Durham

*	15	Darlington Railway Museum (UC)
*	$7\frac{1}{4}$	Hurworth Grange, Hurworth, Darlington (CT)
*	$9\frac{1}{2}$	Lakeshore RR, South Marine Park, South Shields
	$7\frac{1}{4}$	Poacher's Pocket, Metal Bridge, Ferryhill
*	$7\frac{1}{4}$	Roker Park, Sunderland (CT)
*	$7\frac{1}{4}$	Tees Cottage Pumping Station, Darlington (CT)
	15	Whorlton Lido Railway, Barnard Castle

Essex

*	$10\frac{1}{4}$	Audley End Railway, Audley End House, Saffron Walden
*	$7\frac{1}{4}$	Audley End, Saffron Walden (CT)
	$9\frac{1}{2}$	Barking Railway, Barking Park
*	$7\frac{1}{4}$	Barleylands Visitor Centre, Billericay
*	$10\frac{1}{4}$	Basildon MR, Watt Tyler Country Park, Pitsea
*	$7\frac{1}{4}$	East Anglian Railway Museum, Chappel and Wakes Colne
	$7\frac{1}{4}$	Ilford MRC, Chadwell Heath (CT)
	$10\frac{1}{4}$	Maldon MR, The Promenade, Maldon
*	$7\frac{1}{4}$	Rochford Reservoir Railway, Rochford (CT)
*	$10\frac{1}{4}$	Sutton Hall Railway, Rochford (P/OD)
*	$7\frac{1}{4}$	Waterhouse Lane, Chelmsford (CT)
*	$7\frac{1}{4}$	Waterside Farm, Canvey Island (CT)

Gloucestershire

*	$7\frac{1}{4}$	GWR Museum, Coleford
*	15	Perrygrove Railway, Coleford (the author's own railway)
*	$7\frac{1}{4}$	Oldown Country Park, Thornbury

Hampshire

*	$7\frac{1}{4}$	Bitterne Park, Southampton (CT)
*	$8\frac{1}{4}$	(elevated) Brambridge Park Garden Centre, Eastleigh
*	$7\frac{1}{4}$	Cuckoo Hill Railway, Avon Valley Nurseries, South Gorley
*	$7\frac{1}{4}, 10\frac{1}{4}$	Eastleigh Lakeside Railway
*	$12\frac{1}{4}$	Exbury Gardens Steam Railway, Beaulieu
*	$7\frac{1}{4}$	Hollycombe Steam Collection, Liphook
	15	Marwell Zoo, Colden Common, Winchester
	15	Paultons Park, Ower, Romsey
*	$10\frac{1}{4}$	Royal Victoria Country Park, Netley
	$7\frac{1}{4}$	Wellington Country Park, Riseley

Herefordshire

*	$7\frac{1}{4}$	Hereford SoME, Broomy Hill, Hereford (CT)

Hertfordshire

*	$7\frac{1}{4}$	East Herts MR, Van Hages Garden Centre, Great Amwell (CT)
*	$10\frac{1}{4}$	Knebworth Park MR, Stevenage
	$10\frac{1}{4}$	Paradise Wildlife Park, Broxbourne
	$10\frac{1}{4}$	Vanstones Garden Centre, Codicote, Stevenage
*	$10\frac{1}{4}$	Watford MR, Cassiobury Park, Watford

Kent

*	9	Brogdale Horticultural Trust, Faversham (UC)
*	15	Romney Hythe and Dymchurch Railway
	$7\frac{1}{4}$	Strand MR, Strand Lido, Gillingham
*	$7\frac{1}{4}$	Swanley New Barn Railway, New Barn Park, Swanley

Lancashire (including Manchester and Merseyside)

	15	Blackpool Zoo Park, Blackpool
	$7\frac{1}{4}$	Croxteth Park MR, Croxteth Country Park
	15	Haigh Railway, Haigh Country Park, Wigan
	$10\frac{1}{4}$	Happy Mount Park, Bare, Morecambe
	15	Knowsley Safari Park, Prescot
*	15	Lakeside MR, Southport
*	$7\frac{1}{4}$	Lancaster and Morecambe MES, Cinderbarrow Quarry, Burton-in-Kendal (CT)
	21	Pleasure Beach Railway, Blackpool
*	$7\frac{1}{4}$	Springfield Park, Rochdale (CT)
	$10\frac{1}{4}$	St Annes MR, Seafront, St Annes-on-Sea
*	$7\frac{1}{4}$	Thompson Park, Burnley (CT)
*	$7\frac{1}{4}$	Westby MR, Maple Tree Nursery, Kirkham (CT)
*	15	Windmill Animal Farm, Burscough
*	$7\frac{1}{4}$	Worden Park, Leyland (CT)

Leicestershire

*	$7\frac{1}{4}$	Abbey Park, Leicester (CT)
	$10\frac{1}{4}$	Egerton Park Sportsground, Melton Mowbray
*	$10\frac{1}{4}$	Stapleford MR, Melton Mowbray (P/OD)
	$10\frac{1}{4}$	Twycross Zoo

Lincolnshire

	$7\frac{1}{4}$	Belton House, Belton, Grantham
*	15	Cleethorpes Coast Light Railway, Cleethorpes
*	$10\frac{1}{4}$	Kirkby Green Light Railway, Sleaford (P/OD)
*	$7\frac{1}{4}$	North Scarle, Lincoln (CT)
	$7\frac{1}{4}$	Queen's Park, Mablethorpe
*	$7\frac{1}{4}$	Stockholes Farm MR, Belton (P/OD)
*	$7\frac{1}{4}$	Waltham Windmill, Grimsby (CT)

London and Middlesex

*	$7\frac{1}{4}$	Ridgeway Park, Chingford (CT)
*	$7\frac{1}{4}$	Roxbourne Park, Eastcote, Rayners Lane (CT)
*	12	Ruislip Lido Railway
*	$10\frac{1}{4}$	Syon Park, Brentford

Norfolk

*	$7\frac{1}{4}$	Barton House Railway, Wroxham
*	$10\frac{1}{4}$, 15	Bressingham Steam Museum, Diss
*	15	Bure Valley Railway, Aylsham–Wroxham
	$10\frac{1}{4}$	Fritton Lake Country World, Fritton
*	$7\frac{1}{4}$	King's Lynn Leisure Centre (CT)
*	$7\frac{1}{4}$	Norton Hill Light Railway, Snettisham (P/OD)
*	$7\frac{1}{4}$	Pentney Park Railway, Narborough (P/OD)
	$10\frac{1}{4}$	Pettit's Animal Adventure Park, Reedham
*	$10\frac{1}{4}$	Wells and Walsingham Light Railway
*	$10\frac{1}{4}$	Wells Harbour Railway

Northamptonshire

*	$7\frac{1}{4}$	Lower Delapre Park, Northampton (CT)

Northumberland

*	15	Heatherslaw Light Railway, Heatherslaw Mill

Nottinghamshire

*	$7\frac{1}{4}$	Notts Railway Heritage Centre, Ruddington (CT)
*	$7\frac{1}{4}$	Papplewick Pumping Station, near Ravenshead (CT)
*	15	Sherwood Forest Light Railway, near Edwinstowe
	$7\frac{1}{4}$	White Post Wonderland Pleasure Park, Farnsfield

Oxfordshire

	15	Blenheim Park Railway, Woodstock
*	7¼	Cutteslowe Park, Oxford (CT)

Somerset

	7¼	Brean Leisure Park
	9½	Clevedon MR, Salthouse Fields
*	7¼	Hunters Rest MR, Clutton
*	7¼	Weston MR, Beach Road, Weston-super-Mare
	15	Wildlife Park, Cricket St Thomas, Chard

Staffordshire

*	7¼	Baggeridge Country Park, Wombourne (CT)
	10¼	Drayton Manor Park, Tamworth (two lines)
*	7¼	Finney Gardens, Bucknall, Stoke-on-Trent
*	7¼	Hilcote Valley Railway, Fletcher's Garden Centre, Eccleshall
*	7¼	Hollybush Garden Centre, Cannock
*	7¼	Little Hay, Lichfield (CT)
*	10¼	Rudyard Lake Railway, Rudyard
*	7¼	Showground, Stafford (CT)
*	7¼	Weston Park Railway, Weston-under-Lizard

Suffolk

	7¼	Felixstowe MR, Sea Road, Felixstowe
	7¼	Pleasurewood Hills, Corton, Lowestoft
*	7¼	Somerleyton Hall

Surrey

*	7¼	Frimley Lodge MR, Frimley Green (CT)
*	7¼	Great Cockcrow Railway, Chertsey
*	7¼	Malden District SoME, Claygate Lane, Thames Ditton (CT)
*	7¼	Merstham Valley Railway, South Merstham (P/OD)
*	7¼	Mill Lane, Leatherhead (CT)
*	12¼	Newchapel Railway, Horne, Horley (P/OD)
*	7¼	Stoke Park, Guildford (CT)
*	7¼	Woking MR Society, Knaphill, Woking (CT)

Sussex

*	7¼	Alexandra Park, Hastings (CT)
*	7¼	Bentley Wildfowl and Motor Museum, Halland, Uckfield (CT)
	7¼	Bolebroke Castle and Lakes Railway, Hartfield
	10¼	Brooklands Pleasure Park, Worthing
*	10¼, 7¼	Chichester and District SoME, Chichester (CT)
*	7¼	Eastbourne MSR, Lottbridge Drove, Eastbourne
*	7¼	Goldsmiths Recreation Ground, Crowborough (CT)
	10¼	Hastings MR, Hastings
	12¼	Littlehampton MR
*	10¼	Manor Railway, Ingfield Manor, Billingshurst (P/OD)
	7¼	Paradise Leisure Park, Newhaven
*	10¼	South Downs Light Railway, Garden Centre, Pulborough
	10¼	Woodland MR, Hotham Park, Bognor Regis

Warwickshire

*	12¼	Ashorne Hall, Warwick
*	7¼	Echills Wood Railway, National Agricultural Centre, Stoneleigh (P/OD)
*	7¼	Marconi Sports and Social Club, Coventry (CT)
*	7¼	Rainsbrook Valley Railway, Onley Lane, Rugby (CT)

Wiltshire

*	7¼	Coate Water Park, Swindon (CT)
*	15	Longleat Railway, Longleat House
	10¼	Smokey Oak Railway, Woodland Park, Brokerswood, Westbury

Worcestershire

*	7¼	Birmingham Transport Museum, Wythall (CT)
*	7¼	Cherry Orchard, Worcester (CT)
*	7¼	Coalyard MR, Kidderminster

*	7¼	Eckington NGR, Eckington, Pershore
*	15	Evesham Country Park, Evesham (UC)
*	7¼	Leasowes Park, Halesowen
	15	West Midlands Safari Park, Bewdley

Yorkshire

*	7¼	Abbeydale Road South, Dore, Sheffield (CT)
	15	Flamingoland Park, Kirby Misperton
*	7¼	Greenhead Park, Huddersfield (CT)
*	7¼	Hob Moor, Dringhouses, York (CT/UC)
*	15	Kirklees Light Railway, Clayton West (also 7¼ CT)
	15	Lightwater Valley Theme Park, North Stainley, Ripon
	7¼	National Railway Museum, York
*	10¼	Newby Hall MR, Skelton-on-Ure, Ripon
	20	North Bay Railway, Scarborough
*	7¼	Bradford SoME, Northcliffe Woods, Shipley (CT)
*	7¼	Old School, Gilling East (CT)
*	10¼	Orchard Farm Holiday Village, Hunmanby
	7¼	Pugneys Light Railway, Country Park, Wakefield
*	7¼	Ravensprings Park, Brighouse (CT)
*	7¼	Royds Park, Cleckheaton (CT)
*	7¼	Ruswarp MR, Whitby
	15	Saltburn MR, Cat Nab
	10¼	Saville Bros Garden Centre, Garforth
*	10¼	Shibden Park, Halifax
*	7¼	Teesside Small Gauge Railway, Preston Park, Eaglescliffe (CT)
*	7¼	Thorne Park, Thorne, Doncaster (CT)
*	7¼	Thornes Park, Wakefield (CT)
*	7¼	Victoria Park, Rawmarsh (CT)
	12¼	Walkleys Canalside Mill, Hebden Bridge
*	7¼	West Riding Steam Locomotive Society, Blackgates, Tingley, Wakefield (CT)
*	7¼	Wortley Forge, Stocksbridge (CT)

Channel Islands

	7¼	Alderney MR, Alderney
	7¼	Saumarez MR, St Martin, Guernsey

Isle of Man

*	7¼	Curragh Wildlife Park, Ballaugh, Ramsey (CT)

Northern Ireland

*	7¼	Belfast and County Down MR, Donaghadee (CT)
	7¼	Carnfunnock Country Park, Larne, Co. Antrim
	10¼	Delamont Country Park, Killyleagh, Co. Down
	7¼	Pickie Family Fun Park, Bangor, Co. Down
*	7¼	Turnakibbock, Coleraine, Co. Londonderry (CT)
*	7¼	Ulster Folk and Transport Museum, Cultra, Co. Down (CT)

Republic of Ireland

	7¼	J. F. Kennedy Arboretum, New Ross, Co. Wexford
	15	Leisureland Express, Salthill, Galway
*	7¼	Marley Park, Dublin (CT/UC)
	15	Tramore MR, Co. Waterford
	15	Westport House, Knock, Co. Mayo

Scotland

	7¼	Agnew Park, Stranraer
*	7¼	Barshaw Park, Paisley, Renfrew (CT)
*	7¼	Beveridge Park, Kirkcaldy, Fife (CT)
	10¼	Brechin Castle Garden Centre, Brechin, Angus (unconfirmed)
	15	Craigtoun Park, St Andrews, Fife
*	10¼	Kerrs MR, West Links Park, Arbroath, Angus
*	10¼	Lochfyne MR, Ardrishaig, Argyll
*	10¼	Mull and West Highland NGR, Craignure, Isle of Mull
*	7¼	Ness Islands Railway, Whin Park, Inverness
*	7¼	Sanday LR, Sanday, Orkney Islands

*	7¹/₄	Strathaven MR, George Allen Park, Strathaven, Strathclyde
*	7¹/₄	Vogrie Country Park, Newton Grange, Midlothian (CT)

Wales

	7¹/₄	Aberaeron Wildlife and Pleasure Park, Ceredigion
*	9¹/₂	Afon Argoed Country Park, Port Talbot (UC)
*	7¹/₄	Conwy Valley Railway Museum, Betws-y-Coed, Conwy (also 15)
*	7¹/₄	Dibleys Nurseries, Ruthin
*	12¹/₄	Fairbourne and Barmouth Railway, Gwynedd
*	7¹/₄	Gwili Railway, Llwyfan Cerrig, Carmarthenshire
*	7¹/₄, 18	Heath Park, Cardiff (CT)
	15	Oakwood Adventure Park, Narberth, Pembrokeshire
*	7¹/₄	Old Station, Tintern, Monmouthshire (CT)
*	7¹/₄	The Park, Newtown, Powys (CT)
	15	Rhiw Valley Light Railway, Manafon, Powys (P/OD)
*	15	Rhyl MR, Marine Lake, Rhyl, Denbighshire

When you visit a miniature railway, keep any pictures that you take or postcards and guidebooks that you buy. Many lines are here today, gone tomorrow – sometimes without any warning. Subsequently, any mementoes of the line can become valuable. This picture was taken on the 7¹/₄" gauge Little Hereford Light Railway, which no longer exists.

Further reading

Some guidebooks for individual railways and publications that are now out of print have been omitted due to limitations of space. Books on miniature railways are often unavailable through bookshops but the following are specialists (by appointment only):

Andrew Neale Specialist Bookseller, and Plateway Press, 7 Vinery Road, Leeds LS4 2LB. Telephone: 0113 275 8314.

Adrian Sant's Miniature Railway Book and Artefact Emporium, Latch House, Fairmile, Christchurch, Dorset BH23 2UD. Telephone: 01202 474779. Email: sales@miniature-railway-books.com

Bassett-Lowke, Janet. *Bassett-Lowke: A Memoir of His Life and Achievements.* Rail Romances, 1999.
Bluecoaster. *Romney Hythe and Dymchurch Railway, The World's Smallest Public Railway: A Picture Postcard Journey.* Plateway Press, 1987.
Booth, Steve. *Master Railroad Builder.* Paragon Productions, 1992.
Boyd, James. *Don't Stand Up in the Tunnel! The Story of the Downs Light Railway and Its Young Engineers 1925–2001.* Rail Romances, 2001.
Buck, Stan. *Sian and Katie: The Twining Sisters.* Sian Project Group, 1995.
Bullock, Ken. *H.C.S. Bullock, His Life and Locomotives.* Plateway Press/Heywood Society, 1987.
Butterell, Robin. *Miniature Railways.* Ian Allan, 1966.
Butterell, Robin. *Steam on Britain's Miniature Railways: 7¹/₄" to 15" Gauge.* Bradford Barton, 1976.
Butterell, Robin. *The Shillingstone Light Railway.* Robin Butterell, 2000.
Butterell, Robin, Holroyde, Dave, and Townsend, Simon. *ABC Miniature Railways.* Ian Allan, second edition 2000.
Cagney's Locomotive Works. Plateway Press, 1998. (Facsimile catalogue.)

Clarke, Jeremy. *Great Cockcrow Railway*. Ian Allan, 1995.

Clayton, H. *Duffield Bank and Eaton Railways*. Oakwood Press, 1968.

Clayton, Howard, Butterell, Robin, and Jacot, Michael. *Miniature Railways Volume 1: 15 Inch Gauge*. Oakwood Press, 1970.

Croft, D. J. *A Survey of Seaside Miniature Railways*. Oakwood Press, 1992.

Davies, W. J. K. *Ravenglass and Eskdale Railway*. Atlantic, 2000. (Originally published by David & Charles, 1968.)

Davies, W. J. K. *Romney Hythe and Dymchurch Railway*. David & Charles, second edition 1988.

Guy, Keith. *Poole Park Railway: The First 50 Years, 1949–1999*. Friends of Poole Park Railway, 1999.

Health and Safety Executive. *Safe Operation of Miniature Railways, Traction Engines and Road Vehicles* (code ETIS 12). Health and Safety Executive, 2000. (Free – apply to 01787 881165.)

Health and Safety Executive. *Passenger-Carrying Miniature Railways – Guidance on Safe Practice* (code HSG 216). Health and Safety Executive, 2001.

Heywood, Sir Arthur. *Minimum Gauge Railways*. Originally published privately in 1881. Reprints in 1894, 1898 and 1976.

Household, Humphrey. *Narrow Gauge Railways: England and the Fifteen Inch*. Alan Sutton, 1989. (Republished by the Promotional Reprint Company, 1995.)

James, P. *Louis Shaw: Pioneer of 7¼ in Gauge*. 7¼" Gauge Society, 1988.

Jenner, David, and van Zeller, Peter. *Ravenglass and Eskdale Stockbook*. R&ERPS, second edition 1990. (A detailed list of locomotives and rolling stock.)

Jenner, P., Smith, A., and van Zeller, P. *The Ravenglass and Eskdale Railway: A Journey Through Historic Postcards*. The Ravenglass and Eskdale Railway Preservation Society Ltd, 1991.

Kitchenside, Geoffrey. *A Source Book of Miniature and Narrow Gauge Railways*. Ward Lock, 1981.

Knight, Neville. *British Miniature Railways*. Rail Romances, 1999.

Lambert, Arthur. *Miniature Railways Past and Present*. David & Charles, 1982.

Little, Lawson. *Kerr's Miniature Railway: Scotland's Oldest Small-Scale Line*. Narrow Gauge Railway Society, 2000.

McGowan Gradon, W. *'Ratty': The History of the Ravenglass and Eskdale Railway*. Plateway Press, second revised edition 1997. (Originally published 1947.)

Milner, W. J. *Rails through the Sand: The Fairbourne Railway*. Rail Romances, 1996.

Mitchell, Peter, Townsend, Simon, and Shelmerdine, Malcolm. *The Surrey Border and Camberley Railway*. Plateway Press, 1993.

Mosley, David, and van Zeller, Peter. *Fifteen Inch Gauge Railways*. David & Charles, 1986.

Neale, Andrew. *Narrow Gauge and Miniature Railways: From Old Picture Postcards*. Plateway Press, 1986.

R&ER. *Ravenglass and Eskdale Handbook*. R&ER, seventh edition, 1995.

Scott, Peter. *Minor Railways*. Branch Line Society. (Published annually.)

Shaw, Frederic. *Little Railways of the World*. Howell North, 1958.

Simms, Wilfrid. *The Littlehampton Miniature Railway: Golden Jubilee 1948–1998*. W. F. Simms, 1998.

Smithers, Mark. *Sir Arthur Heywood and the Fifteen Inch Gauge Railway*. Plateway Press, 1995.

Snell, J. B. *One Man's Railway: J. E. P. Howey and the Romney Hythe and Dymchurch Railway*. David & Charles, 1983.

Steel, E. A. and E. H. *Miniature World of Henry Greenly*. MAP, 1973.

Strauss, Dr Walter. *Liliputbahnen: A Survey of Passenger-Carrying Miniature Railways*. Robin Butterell, 1988. (Originally published in Germany by Kichler, 1938.)

Tidmarsh, J.G. *The Sutton Coldfield Fifteen Inch Gauge Railway*. Plateway Press, 1990.

van Zeller, Peter. *The Eskdale Railway: A Pictorial Study of 'La'al Ratty'*. Dalesman, 1985.

Vaughan, Adrian. *The History of Bure Valley Railway*. BVRCo, 2000.

Wadey, Mike. *Between the Fires: Eastbourne Miniature Steam Railway*. Mike Wadey, 1998.

White, Roland. *Cromar White Ltd: Miniature Railway Engineers*. Cromar White Developments Ltd, 1991.

Whitehouse, Pat, and Adams, John. *History of Model and Miniature Railways*. Hamlyn–Nel, 1976. (Partwork.)

The *Railway Modeller* magazine usually includes an excellent annual visitors' guide in its June issue each year, often with details of many public miniature railways.

Societies, clubs and magazines

In addition to the following national societies there are numerous model-engineering clubs in many towns and cities.

The **Branch Line Society** encourages the study of railway systems with particular reference to branch lines and minor railways. Principal publication: twice-weekly newsletter *Branch Line News*. Membership Secretary: Rose Grove, 23 Church View, Gillingham, Dorset SP8 4XE. Website: www.branchline.org.uk Details of how to buy *Minor Railways* can be obtained by sending a stamped addressed envelope to 93 Josephine Court, Southcote Road, Reading, Berkshire RG30 2DQ.

The **Narrow Gauge Railway Society** has been serving those who are interested in narrow gauge railways since 1951. Principal publications: *Narrow Gauge News* (bi-monthly) and *The Narrow Gauge* (quarterly); both include plenty of material about miniature railways. Membership Secretary: 15 Highfields Drive, Old Bilsthorpe, Newark NG22 8SN. Website: www.ngrs.org

The **7¹/₄" Gauge Society** is probably the largest miniature railway society in the United Kingdom. Principal publication: *7¹/₄" Gauge News* (quarterly) – an excellent magazine, which is a particularly good source of trade advertisements. Membership Secretary: 115 Tom Lane, Sheffield S10 3PE. Website: www.sevenandaquartergaugesociety.com

The **Heywood Society** covers all miniature railway gauges. Membership is limited by number. Publication: The *Journal* is produced twice each year and is available to non-members from: The Heywood Society Journal, Drummond M. Randall, Birchley, Biddenden, Kent TN27 8DZ. Website: www.rhylminiaturerailway.co.uk

Other publications include:

Grand Scales Quarterly – an excellent publication, edited and published by Greg Robinson. Produced in the United States but with worldwide content on all manner of miniature railways from 12" gauge upwards. The best means of contact is via the website: www.grandscales.com

The *Model Engineer, Engineering in Miniature, Steam Railway* and *Railway Magazine* – four magazines that sometimes cover miniature railways. They can be purchased from newsagents.

Websites

The following sites are limited to those based in the United Kingdom. An evening spent exploring the links from these sites to other sites in Europe and overseas will reveal a cornucopia of miniature lines in almost every country of the world. The sites listed cover the United Kingdom miniature railway scene extremely well, and there is a reasonable probability that they will continue to be available. However, as they are all maintained privately by the owners as a hobby and some are based on free server space, their survival cannot be guaranteed.

groups.yahoo.com Amongst the Yahoo discussion groups are several devoted to miniature railways, including *UKminiaturerailways*. Membership of this group is an excellent way of learning what is happening in the miniature railway field and the author has received considerable help from many of its members.

www.rhylminiaturerailway.co.uk This includes the miniature railway website of Simon Townsend and is outstanding because its author speaks with authority on the subject and maintains an excellent links page.

web.ukonline.co.uk/pe.scott (NB: do not use prefix 'www.') The private site of the compiler of *Minor Railways* provides valuable news items on miniature railway openings and closures.

www.sharpos-world.co.uk If the pictures in this book have whetted your appetite for more of the same, this is a good place to start – go to the miniature railways section.

freespace.virgin.net/ian.thomas1 (NB: do not use prefix 'www.') A good private view of the miniature railway scene.

www.members.tripod.com/minrlylinkspage/index.htm Another good private site.

www.MiniatureRailwaysBook.info The author's own site.

Index